KV-577-353

Local Government

London: H M S O

Researched and written by Publishing Services, Central Office of Informatio

© Crown copyright 1996
Applications for reproduction should be made to HMSO, The Copyright U
St Clements House, 2–16 Colegate, Norwich NR3 1BQ

ISBN 0 11 702037 0

HMSO publications are available from:

HMSO Publications Centre
(Mail, fax and telephone orders only)
PO Box 276, London SW8 5DT
Telephone orders 0171 873 9090
General enquiries 0171 873 0011
(queuing system in operation for both numbers)
Fax orders 0171 873 8200

HMSO Bookshops
49 High Holborn, London WC1V 6HB
(counter service only)
0171 873 0011   Fax 0171 831 1326
68–69 Bull Street, Birmingham B4 6AD
0121 236 9696   Fax 0121 236 9699
33 Wine Street, Bristol BS1 2BQ
0117 926 4306   Fax 0117 9294515
9–21 Princess Street, Manchester M60 8AS
0161 834 7201   Fax 0161 833 0634
16 Arthur Street, Belfast BT1 4GD
01232 238451   Fax 01232 235401
71 Lothian Road, Edinburgh EH3 9AZ
0131 228 4181   Fax 0131 229 2734
The HMSO Oriel Bookshop
The Friary, Cardiff CF1 4AA
01222 395548   Fax 01222 384347

HMSO's Accredited Agents
(see Yellow Pages)

and through good booksellers

Contents

Acknowledgments

This book has been compiled with the help of a number of organisations, including other government departments. The Central Office of Information would like to thank in particular the Department of the Environment, the Department for Education and Employment, the Department of Health, the Home Office, the Department of Social Security, the Department of Transport, and the Northern Ireland Office, The Scottish Office and the Welsh Office.

Introduction

Local government plays a very important role in the lives of many people in Britain.[1] Most schools are still run by local authorities, approximately a quarter of the population live in homes provided by their local authority, and everyone benefits from services such as refuse collection, street lighting and highway maintenance. However, the role and position of local authorities is not static; recent years have seen important changes, with local government taking over some important new functions and losing others.

The structure and financing of local authorities are also in transition. New single-tier or 'unitary' authorities took over from the previous two-tier systems in Scotland and Wales in April 1996. In England, changes are being implemented in many areas following recommendations from the Local Government Commission (see p. 14). In Great Britain the long-established system of local taxation, the rates, was replaced first by the community charge—in England and Wales in 1990—and then by the council tax (see p. 63) in 1993. Developments such as compulsory competitive tendering (CCT—see p. 16) have affected the way that councils deliver their various services to the local electorate. The Government is now encouraging local councils to see themselves increasingly as 'enabling authorities'—arranging for services to be provided to local people without necessarily carrying them out themselves.

---

[1] The term 'Britain' is used informally in this book to mean the United Kingdom of Great Britain and Northern Ireland. 'Great Britain' comprises England, Scotland and Wales.

Origins of Local Government

Local government goes back a very long time in British history, albeit in forms very different from today's. Many old cities have a long and proud tradition of municipal self-government. This is reflected in some of the terminology—for example, the title of alderman[2] dates back to Anglo-Saxon times, and its sense relating to municipal leaders goes back at least to the 13th century. Likewise, the title of mayor, which is still widely used for the presiding officer of councils in England and Wales, also dates back in this meaning at least to the 13th century.

Boroughs

From at least the 12th century, cities received privileges by royal charter—Norwich, for example, has two, dating back to 1158 and 1194. Oxford has a charter dating back to 1191 and a continuous list of mayors and aldermen going back to 1272. Towns that had received the privilege of self-government through royal charter become known as 'boroughs', or 'burghs' in Scotland. Both words derived from the Anglo-Saxon word *burh*, originally simply meaning a fortified town. From the 13th century onwards, boroughs also had the privilege of sending representatives to Parliament. This system eventually fell into disrepute—boroughs such as Old Sarum continued to elect members of Parliament after becoming

---

[2] Aldermen were senior members of a local council elected onto the council by the other councillors and for a longer term than usual. The position was abolished in most areas as part of the local government reforms of the 1970s, although it survives in the City of London. The position of 'bailies' in Scotland was similar.

almost totally deserted (the so-called 'rotten boroughs'), while the new cities of the industrial revolution, lacking the status of boroughs, had no members of Parliament despite their large populations. This eventually led to the Reform Acts of the 19th century.[3]

Counties

Certain matters were dealt with at the level of the shire counties. For example, in Elizabethan times the militias that were the country's prime defence were organised county by county. Likewise, Justices of the Peace were organised by county to try minor offenders, and the assizes, where more serious cases were dealt with, were also held on a county basis.

Parishes

The parishes, into which the country was divided for ecclesiastical purposes, played a part in some of the functions that later fell to local authorities. Probably the most important among these was relief of the poor. Starting with the Poor Law of 1601, those who were deemed 'sturdy beggars' (able-bodied beggars judged capable of working) were severely punished, but those who were felt to be incapable of supporting themselves were helped by the parish, which had to appoint an Overseer of the Poor. A 'rate' (see p. 61) was charged on householders to pay for poor relief. From 1723 onwards, parishes were empowered to set up workhouses where the able-bodied poor could be set to work. Likewise, each parish chose its constable responsible for maintaining order and also for road repairs. The ecclesiastical origin of the parish system was reflected

[3] See *Parliamentary Elections* (Aspects of Britain: HMSO, 1995).

in the title of 'vestry', the committee which organised such services.

Nineteenth Century Reforms

The industrial revolution and the great expansion of many cities created problems which the existing structures could not cope with. For example, the old church graveyards became full and could no longer provide sanitary burial space; diseases such as cholera, carried by tainted drinking water, became common, and better policing was needed to maintain order. A series of legislative reforms were passed to address these problems.

The Municipal Corporations Act 1835, which applied to England and Wales, required most of the existing boroughs to have councils properly elected by the ratepayers and to open their meetings to the public. There were also a number of other bodies set up for specific purposes. For example, the Education Act 1870 provided for school boards to be set up where school provision was inadequate or where local ratepayers requested it. Such boards were to be supported from the rates and had powers to compel the attendance of pupils at school. Likewise, health authorities were established throughout England and Wales under the Public Health Act 1872. Their responsibilities were not those of modern-day health authorities; rather, their primary role was the improvement of sanitary conditions.

The Local Government Act 1888 set up county councils. These looked after functions such as highways and police. However, larger towns—those with populations of 50,000 or more—could set up county borough councils, which were all-purpose authorities independent of the county councils. Smaller boroughs remained as non-county boroughs under the counties.

The Local Government Act 1894 created urban district councils and rural district councils for those areas within county council jurisdiction which did not have borough status.

From 1888, the top tier of local government in London was provided by the creation of the London County Council. The area of this was, however, considerably smaller than today's Greater London. Under the London Government Act 1899, the metropolitan borough councils were established to take over the more local functions. These boroughs were considerably smaller in area than today's London boroughs. The City of London retained responsibility for its area.

From 1834 onwards, parishes began to be grouped together into unions, each with a Board of Guardians, for discharging their poor law responsibilities; this in effect created a distinction between civil and ecclesiastical parishes. The Local Government Act 1894 created parish councils in something like their modern form.

Although at first many of these councils had fairly limited responsibilities, they rapidly acquired many of the powers hitherto vested in separate bodies. For example, county councils took over education from school boards in 1902; this remains today the largest and most expensive local government function. Local authorities also acquired new powers, such as the power to build low-cost housing and the power to exert some control over the development of land.

Scotland

Local government development in Scotland followed a broadly similar path during the 19th century, with the burghs being reformed by Act of Parliament and boards set up for various purposes, such as education. The system was not finally rationalised until 1929, when it came to comprise four all-purpose 'counties of cities'—similar to county boroughs in England and Wales—and 33 counties. Under the counties were large burghs (responsible for most local government functions), small burghs (with much more limited responsibilities) and district councils.

Public Utilities

In the 19th century, local authorities also began to acquire a role in the provision of public utilities. Gas (at first primarily for lighting) was often supplied by municipal rather than private undertakings, to the extent that the artificial gas made from coal used until the advent of natural gas in the 1970s was often known as 'town gas'. The Electric Lighting Act 1882 allowed the Board of Trade to grant exclusive rights to supply consumers with electricity in a given area, and a large part of the industry came to be provided by local authorities. Water services, too, were often provided by local authorities. By the end of the Second World War, about four-fifths of water supply and one third of gas supply were in municipal hands.

In Kingston-upon-Hull the telephone service was provided by the local authority, which retained it even after 1912 when the remainder of Britain's telephones came under the control of the General Post Office. Kingston Communications is still owned by the council, although with the liberalisation of the telecommunications market, it no longer has a local monopoly.

Twentieth Century Changes

Although the 19th century reforms had established the basic framework of local government, the structure was not static. There was considerable pressure from district councils in medium-sized towns to adopt county borough status, which many of them did, while other district councils merged to form larger units.

Particularly in the years after the Second World War, local government began to lose some of its traditional functions. Electricity and gas were nationalised in 1948 and 1949 respectively, and so local authorities lost their role in supplying these utility services. Water supply functions in England and Wales were transferred in the 1970s to water authorities, although in Scotland water remained a local authority responsibility.[4] Likewise, the creation of the National Health Service meant that the health functions that local authorities had built up were lost to them over a period of time. The National Health Service Act 1946 transferred local authority hospitals to health authorities, but left local authorities responsible for the ambulance service, health visitors and the prevention of illness. These, too, were later transferred. The relief of the poor, which had been a county function since the abolition of the Boards of Guardians in 1929, was transferred to central government with the establishment of the National Assistance Board. Increasingly it was felt that the structure of local government was overdue for major reform, and the question began to be examined.

[4] This changed in April 1996—see p. 23.

Developments in Recent Years

The 1960s and 70s saw considerable change in the organisation of local government, with major structural reform taking place after considerable debate. The metropolitan areas saw further change in the 1980s.

The 1965 Reforms in London

In 1965 London government was reformed. The Greater London Council (GLC) replaced the London County Council (LCC), embracing a much larger area than had previously been covered by the LCC. The GLC had responsibility for various services, such as strategic planning, the fire brigade and public transport. It also provided housing alongside the boroughs. Within the GLC area, 32 boroughs and the City of London were responsible for many services. Many of these boroughs were formed by the amalgamation of existing smaller boroughs. For example, the metropolitan borough of Camberwell (see Appendix 1, pp. 81–6) was combined with the boroughs of Southwark and Bermondsey to form the London borough of Southwark. In the outer parts of London, the boroughs also had responsibility for education. A separate Inner London Education Authority (ILEA) was established to cover education in the inner boroughs; the GLC councillors elected for those areas served on it, along with others appointed by the boroughs themselves.

Redcliffe-Maud Report

A Royal Commission to look at local government in England outside London was established in 1966 and reported in 1969. Its report, known as the Redcliffe-Maud report, suggested a thorough reform of the existing structure. It recommended a structure consisting of:

— three metropolitan areas (Birmingham, Liverpool and Manchester) with a strategic authority akin to the GLC and several district councils under it;

— 58 new unitary authorities covering other areas; and

— eight provincial councils, mostly elected by the unitary and metropolitan authorities, to decide the strategic framework of social and economic development in their areas.

These proposed local authorities generally represented a considerable increase in size from the then existing boroughs, this being felt to allow more efficient local government.

In the event, the proposed structure attracted criticism in various quarters and was not adopted. The Government published its own proposals in 1971, accepting the idea of metropolitan county councils but rejecting the idea of unitary authorities. Slightly modified, these proposals formed the basis of the reforms introduced under the Local Government Act 1972.

The 1974 Reforms in England and Wales

Local government in England and Wales outside London was reformed with the introduction of a new structure in April 1974 under the provisions of the Local Government Act 1972.[5] The system consisted of two tiers: county councils and district councils. In the 1960s and 1970s it was felt that for some services it was more administratively or economically efficient for local authorities to cover wide areas or serve many people. On the other hand, it was believed that those services closely tailored to the specific needs of individual communities were best organised through smaller units, which could be closer to the electorate. Accordingly, functions were allocated to two main tiers of local authority.

The county boundaries, which dated back to medieval times, were reformed. Some counties were merged—for example Herefordshire and Worcestershire—while others were split—for example Sussex. Several new counties were created from parts of existing counties—for example, Avon was created by detaching the parts of Somerset and Gloucestershire nearest Bristol from their original counties and making a new county out of them. In other areas the boundaries were adjusted—for example a large part of Berkshire was transferred to Oxfordshire. In particular, six new metropolitan county councils (rather than the three proposed by the Redcliffe-Maud report) were created in large conurbations— Greater Manchester, Merseyside, South Yorkshire, Tyne and Wear, West Midlands and West Yorkshire. In Wales a new set of counties was created, mostly combining old counties into larger ones but in the case of the heavily populated Glamorgan area splitting it into three. Many people, however, disliked the new boundaries and preferred the traditional ones. The unpopularity of new counties such as Avon was one of the factors that led to the

[5] This Act not only set up the new structure, it also systematised the procedural rules for the conduct of local authority business.

establishment of the Local Government Commission for England to review the structure again (see p. 14). Within each county, a number of district councils were set up. The number of districts per county varied, with the Isle of Wight and South Glamorgan each having only two, and Essex having no fewer than 17. Between five and eight districts, however, was typical. The district councils took responsibility for various services, generally those where it was felt that a smaller organisation could provide the service effectively. The sorts of service that the county councils provided tended to be those for which a larger area was needed, such as strategic planning, or where it was felt that a smaller body could not provide the service effectively, such as education.

Scotland

A Royal Commission on local government in Scotland reported in 1969. It proposed seven regional authorities responsible for most major services, and 37 district authorities responsible for a wide range of other services.

The reforms actually adopted varied from this slightly— in the event nine regions and 53 districts were established. The division of responsibilities was broadly similar to that in England and Wales. Three unitary islands councils—Orkney, Shetland and Western Isles—were also set up.

Northern Ireland

In the 1960s Northern Ireland was the only part of Britain to have what might be termed a regional tier of government, with its own parliament sitting at Stormont. There were also six county councils, two county boroughs, nine boroughs, 25 urban districts and 26 rural districts. Following the outbreak of the troubles in the late 1960s, this structure was abolished in 1973. A review body to look at the structure of local government was set up in 1969, and reported in 1970. It recommended up to 26 elected district councils to administer local services, with regional services the responsibility of the ministries that were responsible to the Stormont parliament. The day-to-day running of these services should be decentralised to delegated boards.

Legislation in 1972 laid the foundations for this, with 26 district councils being set up to replace the 73 existing local authorities. The first elections for the new councils were held in May 1973, with the new councils coming into being later in that year. Their responsibilities include local environmental services such as street cleaning, cemeteries and food hygiene. With the disappearance of the Stormont parliament, the regionally-administered services are answerable to the Secretary of State for Northern Ireland.

Abolition of Metropolitan County Councils

The Local Government Act 1985 abolished the GLC and the six metropolitan county councils. Their functions were transferred in April 1986 to the London boroughs and metropolitan district councils respectively and to some other public bodies. The London Fire and Civil Defence Authority and the London Waste Regulation Authority were established to take over those functions in the capital. At first the ILEA retained its functions and became a directly-elected authority. However, it too was abolished in 1990 when the inner London boroughs took on responsibility for education. In the six metropolitan county areas joint authorities were established to run county-wide functions. Responsibility for other county services was transferred either to the districts, or, on a short-term basis, to the residuary bodies which were set up to settle the affairs of the abolished councils.

Table 1 shows the most heavily populated district councils in Britain.

Table 1: Most Populated District Councils in Britain, 1993

	Population ('000)	Area (sq km)
Birmingham	1,012	265
Leeds	725	562
Glasgow City	682	198
Sheffield	532	367
Bradford	480	366
Liverpool	477	113
Edinburgh City	441	261
Manchester	432	116
Bristol	398	110
Kirklees	386	410
Wirral	334	159
Croydon	323	87
Wakefield	318	333
Wigan	313	199
Dudley	312	98
Coventry	304	97
Cardiff	299	120
Sunderland	298	138
Belfast	297	130
Sefton	294	153

Source: *Regional Trends.*

Local Government Reorganisation and Reform

As local government has changed in its approach over recent years—for example through concepts such as the 'enabling authority' (see p. 16)—so the assumption that underpinned the 1970s reforms—that a certain minimum size was needed for the discharge of certain functions—has also been challenged. This in turn has led to greater support for unitary authorities.

Local Government Commission for England

The Local Government Act 1992 established the Local Government Commission for England, with a remit to review the structure, boundaries and electoral arrangements of local government in England and to undertake periodic electoral reviews. So far the majority of its work has been to review the structure of local government in non-metropolitan England. The reviews considered whether the two-tier structure should be retained or whether single-tier ('unitary') authorities would better reflect the identities and interests of local communities and secure effective and convenient local government. For the most part the Commission recommended the retention of two-tier government, but suggested unitary authorities for some areas, especially the larger cities. Most of these recommendations have been accepted by the Secretary of State for the Environment, but in some areas he has asked the Commission to conduct fresh reviews on individual districts.

Following its work on non-metropolitan areas, the Commission will proceed to look at metropolitan districts and London.

The Local Government Commission published its final reports on all the non-metropolitan areas by January 1995. The first change—the establishment of a unitary authority for the Isle of Wight—came into effect in April 1995. With effect from April 1996, the county councils of Avon, Humberside and Cleveland were abolished and a new authority established for the city of York. Other changes will take effect from 1997. The Government has announced a mechanism whereby local authorities can borrow to meet transitional costs.

In 1993 the Government established the Local Government Staff Commission to advise it on staffing matters arising from the reorganisation. It has produced advice on redundancy payments and has issued a circular on the procedures that local authorities should follow for the transfer and recruitment of staff. As with the abolition of the metropolitan counties, a residuary body has also been set up, responsible for selling surplus property and dividing the proceeds among the local authorities involved.

Wales and Scotland

In Wales and Scotland, the Government followed a different approach to the reform of local government structure. Following extensive consultation, the Government legislated through the Local Government etc. (Scotland) Act 1994 and the Local Government (Wales) Act 1994 for the creation of new unitary councils there. There are 29 of these councils in Scotland, in addition to the existing three Islands authorities which now remain, and 22 in Wales.

'Enabling Authorities'

There have been numerous changes in recent years in the way that local authorities approach their responsibilities. Many of these can be encapsulated under the term 'enabling authority'. It is used to describe the general shift away from local authorities providing services directly and towards them arranging for services to be provided, or carrying out functions in partnership with other bodies. For example, councils often have nomination rights to housing association properties (see p. 29), so that they are acting not as provider but as 'gatekeeper'. Likewise, under the community care reforms, councils with social services responsibilities draw up care plans for those who need them (see p. 33), but the care is often provided by the private or voluntary sectors funded by the council, rather than directly by the local authority itself.

Compulsory Competitive Tendering

Many authorities employ their own permanent staff to carry out construction and maintenance work. Where this occurs, the workforce is known as a direct labour organisation (DLO) or direct service organisation (DSO).

In 1980 legislation was introduced to increase the efficiency, competitiveness and accountability of DSOs. It required authorities wishing to carry out certain defined activities above certain cost levels through their own DSO to first expose that work to competitive tender. The legislation also required authorities carrying out work in-house to keep separate financial accounts and to meet specified financial objectives. In 1993–94, some 2,100 out of 2,400 DSOs met their financial targets. However, the Government has various powers if a DSO fails to achieve the target. It can require the authority to account for the loss, and may then take various steps, such as requiring a contract to be retendered or even, in extreme cases, ordering the closure of the DSO. Similar powers exist where competition is prevented, distorted or restricted in order to give the DSO an advantage over its competitors.

The 1980 legislation was a first step towards the consideration of contracting out services to private contractors as a way of making savings. Substantial cost reductions were shown by those councils voluntarily putting out services such as refuse collection, street cleaning and park maintenance to competitive contract. The Government therefore legislated in the Local Government Act 1988 to extend competition in the provision of local authority services. This process, compulsory competitive tendering or CCT, took in various local government services, including:

— refuse collection;

— street cleaning;

— cleaning of buildings;

— schools and welfare catering;

— other catering;

— vehicle maintenance;

— leisure management; and

— grounds maintenance.

CCT was applied to these services in tranches between 1989 and 1994. Minimum proportions of work to be exposed to CCT by certain dates were laid down by the Government, although local authorities had the discretion to introduce competition faster if they chose.

The extent to which contracts have been awarded to outside contractors varies from service to service. The Local Government Management Board estimates that the internal DSOs have won only about 45 per cent of the number of building cleaning contracts (73 per cent by value), but 75 per cent of the number of education and welfare catering contracts (82 per cent by value). The Government estimates that CCT has resulted in a cost saving of 7 per cent since its introduction.

The Government is currently extending the scope of CCT to cover other services, especially in the white-collar area. For example, 45 per cent of legal work has to be put out to tender by April 1996 in the case of London boroughs and metropolitan districts. Other services affected include information technology services, housing management, finance, personnel, and corporate and administrative services. Special arrangements have been made for those authorities which are being affected by reorganisation.

Structure and Functions of Local Government

In non-metropolitan parts of England, the county councils are broadly responsible for matters requiring planning and administration over wide areas or the support of substantial resources. Examples include:

—strategic planning;

—transport planning;

—highways;[6]

—traffic regulation;

—education and libraries;

—consumer protection;

—refuse disposal;

—fire services; and

—personal social services.

District councils generally administer functions of more local significance. Examples are:

—environmental health;

—housing;

—decisions on most planning applications;

[6] The most important routes—trunk roads—are the direct responsibility of the Department of Transport in England and of the Welsh Office in Wales and The Scottish Office in Scotland.

—refuse collection;

—collection of local taxes; and

—off-street car parks (with the consent of the county council concerned).

Museums, art galleries and parks are provided by both types of authority, depending on local agreement.

In London and the other metropolitan areas, a unitary structure was created by the abolition of the GLC and the metropolitan county councils in 1986. Most of the functions previously carried out by the GLC and the metropolitan county councils have been transferred to the London boroughs and the metropolitan district councils respectively. A small number of services requiring a statutory authority over areas wider than the boroughs and districts are run by joint authorities composed of elected councillors nominated by the boroughs or district councils concerned. These included:

—waste regulation[7] and disposal in certain areas;

—the police and fire services, including civil defence, and public transport in all metropolitan counties; and

—the fire service, including civil defence, in London.

The present structure review (see p. 14) will increase the number of unitary councils. The Isle of Wight became a unitary authority in April 1995 and 13 other unitary authorities were set up in April 1996. Twelve of these will replace the existing counties of Avon, Cleveland and Humberside, and the 13th will replace the two-tier structure in York. Further unitary authorities are planned for 1997.

---

[7] Waste regulation functions became the responsibility of the new Environment Agency when this was set up in April 1996.

Table 2: English Local Authorities, 1994–95

Type	Number	Average population	Average area (sq km)
County	39	770,000	3,100
District	296	100,000	400
Metropolitan district	36	310,000	200
London borough	32	200,000	50

Type	Average number of councillors	Average revenue expenditure[a] (£ million)	Average capital expenditure[b] (£ million)
County	77	484	42
District	45	11	8
Metropolitan district	69	244	48
London borough	60	200	41

Source: Department of the Environment.
[a] Budgeted spending. Excludes housing revenue account expenditure.
[b] Forecast gross capital expenditure.

City of London

The historic City of London covers 2.6 sq km (1 sq mile) in the heart of the capital and has a resident population of about 4,000, although some 350,000 people travel into the area to work each weekday. The history, constitution and powers of the Corporation of the City of London are unlike those of any other local authority. It acts, and has acted for centuries, through three courts:

—the Court of Common Council;

—the Court of Aldermen; and

—the Court of Common Hall.

The Lord Mayor of London presides over all three courts. The Court of Aldermen is the only surviving example in England of a municipal second chamber. Aldermen, elected on the basis of the parliamentary register, hold office for life. In the past, the elected aldermen had a decisive influence on the development of civic government, and were usually chosen from among the leading personalities in the City at the time.

The Lord Mayor holds several ancient offices and acts as leading citizen in the City's ceremonial, social and traditional functions. The Corporation performs in the City the normal functions carried out by the borough councils elsewhere in the capital. It is also responsible, through the Lord Mayor, for a number of special diplomatic activities associated with the history and traditions of the City. The City also maintains its own police force.

Wales

Until April 1996, Wales was divided into eight counties, which between them were divided into a total of 37 districts. The division of responsibility between districts and counties was broadly the same as in England; one difference was that waste disposal was a district function, not a county function as in England. After April 1996 the 22 new unitary councils took over (see p. 15); these are responsible for the full range of local government services in Wales.

Scotland

Until April 1996, local government in mainland Scotland was divided between nine regions and 53 districts, with the split being broadly analogous to that in England and Wales. Most functions that in England are carried out by the counties were done in Scotland by the regions. However, there were some differences. For example, libraries were normally provided by the districts (unlike England and Wales), but in three of the more sparsely populated regions they were provided by the regional authorities. There are also three Islands authorities—Orkney, Shetland and Western Isles—which provide the full range of local government services.

As in Wales, 29 new unitary councils came into being in April 1996. These took over all local government functions in their areas. The Islands authorities remained unaffected by this change. The provision of water and sewerage was until then still a local government responsibility in Scotland; however, after the April 1996 reorganisation it was transferred from the regional authorities to three new independent water authorities. A number of local councillors serve on their boards.

Northern Ireland

The principal functions of the 26 district councils are:

—recreation;

—environmental health;

—cleansing and sanitation;

—cemeteries and crematoria;

—building control; and

—markets and abattoirs.

There are four Health and Social Services Boards and five Education and Library boards, a proportion of whose members are district councillors. Fire cover is provided by a single board. Social housing is run by the Northern Ireland Housing Executive. Other services, such as water and sewerage, planning, highways and pollution control, are directly provided by the Northern Ireland Office. Electoral registration and the organisation of all elections are carried out by the Chief Electoral Officer, an independent official appointed by the Government.

Borough and City Status

A district council may petition for a Royal Charter granting 'borough' status to the district. Outside London a total of 172 districts in England and Wales have been granted borough status. The status of 'city', with or without the right to call the mayor 'lord mayor', may be granted by Royal Letters Patent. In London there are the Cities of London and Westminster, and outside London 50 districts have city status, 22 of them having lord mayors. City status is regarded as a considerable honour, and new grants are rare, usually being made to mark a notable occasion. The two most recent in England were to Derby in 1977 to mark the Queen's silver jubilee, and to Sunderland in 1992 to mark the 40th anniversary of her accession. On the latter occasion, several local authorities put themselves forward for consideration before the decision went in favour of Sunderland. The status of borough or city is significant for ceremonial purposes but makes no difference to the administrative functions of the council concerned.

Parishes and Communities

There are over 10,000 civil parishes[8] in England, forming a third and more minor tier of local government. Parishes have operated as units of local government since 1894. Most were not affected by the reorganisation in 1974, except that the powers of parish councils were extended and 300 small towns (former small boroughs and urban districts) became 'successor' parishes, whose councils have the same powers as other parish councils. The minimum parish council size is five councillors.

Some parishes have considerable populations, the largest (Bracknell in Berkshire) having over 50,000. About 2,000 parishes have populations below 200, which are too small to need a parish council. Their affairs are governed by a meeting of all local government electors living in the parish.

All parishes must have parish meetings which all their local government electors are entitled to attend. Where there is a parish council, the parish meeting must take place at least once a year; where there is not, at least twice. Parish councils do not receive any general government grant; they are funded out of the council tax.

Parishes do not have a right to provide specific services but may do so with the agreement of districts or counties. They normally provide and manage local facilities such as village halls, allotments and village greens. Footway lighting is sometimes provided by parish councils. They are also entitled to be consulted by the local planning authority on planning applications in their areas.

A 1991 survey of parish and town councils in England (see Further Reading) found that the average council had nine council-

[8] These are quite distinct from the ecclesiastical parishes of the Church of England.

lors representing a parish of 1,700 people, with a part-time clerk and annual revenue expenditure of £15,000. However, this masks considerable diversity—some have no paid staff at all and are run on an entirely voluntary basis, while others represent communities of over 30,000 people and may have annual budgets of over £1 million.

In Wales, with its different religious traditions, the term 'parish' is not used. Instead, there is provision for community councils, the powers of which are the same as parish councils in England. In Scotland community councils are not a tier of local government, even though they were set up by statute. Their general purpose is to ascertain, co-ordinate and express the views of the communities they represent to local authorities and other public bodies in the area. Although community councils have no statutory responsibility or source of finance, local authorities may provide them with financial and administrative assistance as well as grants related to specific projects.

Parish and community councils may call themselves 'town councils', in which case the presiding councillor is known as the town mayor. There are six parishes in England and one community in Wales with city status and city mayors.

Major Local Government Functions

Airports

A significant number of Britain's smaller airports are municipally-owned, many of them having been developed by local authorities to promote the economic development of their areas. The Government is encouraging the privatisation of local-authority airports. Some seaports are also owned by local councils.

Cemeteries and Crematoria

Local authorities do not have a duty to provide cemeteries and crematoria, although many do so. There is now, however, a trend towards private sector crematoria. There is a duty on local authorities to secure the proper disposal of human remains in their areas if suitable arrangements have not been made by the deceased's family or friends.

Consumer Protection

Trading standards officers protect the public from unscrupulous or unsafe trading practices. For example, in the run-up to Christmas councils often seize cheap imported toys on sale in their areas that do not meet safety standards. Likewise, seizures of cheap and inferior counterfeit goods are common. Complaints from members of the public can be investigated. Trading standards officers have the power to check traders' weights and measures. Trading standards officers are provided by the county councils, the metropolitan districts and London boroughs, and the Scottish regional councils.

Economic Development

Councils are allowed to promote the economic development of their area. This is done in a variety of ways, for example by making grants and loans to small businesses, funding the provision of training courses to improve the job prospects of local people, and providing industrial premises tailored to small businesses. A number of government and European Union (EU) programmes assist local authorities in this role.

Education

Local education authorities[9] provide primary and secondary schooling and special schools for handicapped children. At one time all state schools were funded by the local education authority; however, in recent years there has been provision for schools to become grant-maintained—that is, funded directly by central government and, since April 1994, the Funding Agency for Schools. Nevertheless, local education authorities still provide nearly 3,100 secondary and 18,400 primary schools. In 1995 English local authorities employed 372,600 teachers and lecturers and 262,000 other people in education functions.[10]

Local education authorities are also responsible for paying student grants to people from their area who go to university. In England the local education authorities are the district councils in metropolitan areas, the county councils in non-metropolitan areas and the London boroughs.

Environmental Health

Environmental health is a function of district councils (including those in Northern Ireland), metropolitan districts and London boroughs. These councils have a duty to inspect their areas for 'statutory nuisances' such as dust, smells and noise from business premises; air pollution from potentially less seriously polluting processes is regulated under a system of local authority air pollution control.[11] Restaurants and other premises serving food

---

[9] For more information, see *Education* (Aspects of Britain: HMSO, 1995).
[10] These figures on the number of employees, and the figures that follow, give full-time equivalents.
[11] For more information, see *Pollution Control* (Aspects of Britain: HMSO, 1993).

are inspected for hygiene. Local authorities in England employed 17,600 people in environmental health in 1995.

Fire and Civil Defence

Fire protection is provided by county councils and, in the metropolitan counties, by joint authorities. Especially in rural areas, fire cover is sometimes provided by volunteer firefighters. The standards of fire cover are set by the Home Office. Offices, factories and some residential properties such as hotels require a fire certificate; the local authority checks the premises and may require alterations to improve fire safety before granting the certificate. There were 33,800 people in the regular fire services in England in 1994.

Highways

County councils, metropolitan district councils and London boroughs are the highway authorities for their area. They are responsible for the upkeep and repair of most non-trunk roads (some roads have not been 'adopted' by the local authority and so are private roads). Street lighting, however, is not necessarily provided by the highway authority—some, for example, is provided by parish councils. In London, the boroughs have taken over from the police the responsibility for enforcing parking restrictions.

Housing

District councils, London boroughs and metropolitan district councils are responsible for housing.[12] Most manage rented social housing, although in recent years some have transferred their stock

[12] For more information, see *Housing* (Aspects of Britain: HMSO, 1993).

to housing associations. Housing associations have now become the main providers of new social housing. Housing authorities' powers and duties include:

—dealing with poor housing conditions;

—providing grants to help with repair and improvement of housing;

—housing homeless people in defined priority need, the categories of which include families with young children, pregnant women, and those vulnerable through old age or physical disability;

—advising homeless people who do not qualify for rehousing; and

—administering the housing benefit scheme to help tenants on low incomes with their housing costs (see p. 60).

There were almost 4.7 million recipients of housing benefit in Great Britain in February 1994, 3.0 million of whom were local authority tenants. Total expenditure on housing benefit in 1993–94 came to £8,821 million.

Local housing authorities must maintain a separate housing revenue account (HRA), which is kept separate from the funds used to provide other services. This prevents the council tax being used to subsidise rents or *vice versa*. There were 67,900 housing staff in England in 1995.

A White Paper, *Our Future Homes: Opportunity, Choice, Responsibility*, published in June 1995, proposes various reforms to the housing system, including:

—changes to the allocations system to remove disadvantage from people on the waiting list who may be in housing need but do not meet the statutory criteria for homelessness;

—the introduction of probationary tenancies, so that councils could take action against anti-social tenants; and

—making stronger powers available to local authorities to deal with the safety of houses in multiple occupation.

Leisure

The provision of facilities such as parks, swimming pools and sports centres is a discretionary power rather than a duty for local authorities. However, because these facilities are greatly prized by local residents, provision is widespread, usually at the district council level. In recent years, the facilities have improved at many leisure centres, with pools often incorporating water slides and wave machines, and facilities being provided for a wide range of other sports and exercise, such as squash, badminton and aerobics. The nature conservation role of the open spaces maintained by local authorities has increasingly been recognised.

Libraries

Some councils have a statutory duty to provide a comprehensive library service. In England and Wales, libraries are provided by county councils, metropolitan districts and London boroughs. In Scotland, the library service is provided partly by regional councils and partly by district councils. There were 30,900 library, museum and art gallery staff in England in 1995.

Planning

London boroughs and the metropolitan district councils are responsible for land use planning[13] in their areas. Elsewhere in

---

[13] For more information, see *Planning* (Aspects of Britain: HMSO, 1992).

England and Wales planning functions are divided between county and district councils. County councils are responsible for county-wide structure plans setting a broad framework for development control. They also deal with applications for mineral development and (except in Wales) for the disposal of waste. District councils deal with most local plans and decide all other applications for planning permission. The National Parks authorities—at one time mostly joint committees of the relevant local authorities but put on a statutory basis by the Environment Act 1995—act as planning authorities for their areas. There were 25,400 planning and economic development staff in England in 1995.

Police

Outside London many counties have their own police under a police authority, though several counties have combined forces. The police authority, which sets policy, is a committee which includes local county councillors and magistrates; operational decisions are in the hands of the senior police officers. In London the Metropolitan Police is the responsibility of the Home Secretary. It covers all of Greater London, with the exception of the City, and certain adjacent areas. In 1994 in England there were 121,000 police officers of all ranks and 46,900 civilian employees in the police service.

Public Transport

In the metropolitan counties, passenger transport authorities, through passenger transport executives, are responsible for local bus and rail subsidies, and for organising concessionary fare schemes. Members of the authorities are largely nominated by local government. Local authorities elsewhere can subsidise socially necessary bus services. Outside London, district councils are responsible for licensing taxis.

Social Services

County councils, metropolitan district councils and London boroughs have social services responsibilities.[14] Traditionally this has typically included the provision of:

—day centres and social clubs for elderly people;

—'meals-on-wheels' services delivering hot food;

—home helps for elderly and handicapped people;

—day care facilities for children under five; and

—care for socially deprived children through residential homes or foster parents.

Such provision may be made directly or by funding voluntary organisations to provide the service. In 1993 there were 52,000 children looked after by local authorities in England, of whom 32,500 were placed with foster parents. There were 74,800 people supported by local authorities in homes for the elderly or the physically disabled; the vast majority of these people were aged 65 or over. At that time, most of the places were in local authority-run homes. There were 245,900 social services staff in England in 1995.

In recent years social services responsibilities have been greatly broadened by the introduction of 'community care' provisions. Authorities with social services responsibilities now have a duty to provide a 'care package' for those who need it; this may include services such as home helps to help elderly or disabled people cope with living at home or funding residential care for those

[14] For more information, see *Social Welfare* (Aspects of Britain: HMSO, 1995).

who are no longer able to stay in their own homes. The Government has made considerable extra funding available to local authorities to help them meet this. These changes will have altered very greatly the figures quoted above for local authority-supported places in homes.

Waste Management

District and borough councils collect household waste and much commercial and industrial waste. Household waste is collected mainly free of charge, although councils can charge for collection of certain types of household waste, such as garden waste or large bulky items. A charge may be made for commercial refuse, and many businesses instead have contracts with private sector companies.

Waste disposal authorities are responsible for waste disposal. In England these are the county councils, metropolitan district and London borough councils (except in Greater Manchester, Merseyside and four areas of London where there are statutory joint waste disposal authorities). However, local authority waste regulation functions were taken over by the Environment Agency in April 1996.

Many local authorities also provide household waste recycling facilities. The number of these facilities has increased considerably. For example, the number of bottle banks rose from 17 in 1977 to nearly 12,700 in 1992 and 17,650 in 1994.

Local Elections and Councillors

The involvement of locally elected councillors is what gives local government its responsiveness to local needs. Councillors have several distinct functions, but ultimately they stem from the councillors' position as the elected representatives of their area.

Elections

Councillors are generally elected for four years. Local elections are normally held on the first Thursday in May, and every year sees a large number of local elections take place. However, not every council has elections every year; in many areas local elections are only held once every four years.

All county councils in England, London borough councils, and about two-thirds of non-metropolitan district councils are elected in their entirety every four years. In the remaining districts (including all metropolitan districts) one-third of the councillors are elected in each of the three years when county council elections are not held. Where new unitary authorities are being set up in England following the Local Government Commission review, the parliamentary orders make the necessary provisions regarding elections.

In Scotland and Wales the first elections to the new councils took place in April and May 1995 respectively. The councillors elected at first formed a 'shadow' authority, which had no power but made preparations for the take-over from the old councils in April 1996. The next local elections are due in 1999, with subsequent elections held every three years in Scotland and four years in Wales. In both cases, these elections cover the whole council at once.

Where a councillor resigns, dies or forfeits office,[15] a by-election is normally held a few weeks later, an exception being where the councillor to be replaced had only a brief time left in office. These by-elections can take place at any time during the year, although like parliamentary elections they are always held on a Thursday. Electors of the relevant ward or division can trigger a by-election where one has not yet been called by giving notice to the relevant council officer, but in practice this is usually done by the political parties represented on the council.

Voters

Anyone may vote at a local government election in Britain provided he or she is:

—aged 18 years or over;

—a citizen of Britain, another Commonwealth country or the Irish Republic, or, from 1996, a citizen of the EU;

—not legally disqualified (which might be as a result of conviction for corrupt or illegal election practices, or imprisonment); and

—on the electoral register.

To qualify for registration, he or she must be resident in the council area on the qualifying date (10 October of each year). The register is compiled annually by the local authority's electoral registration officer. It comes into force on 16 February of the

---

[15] Councillors can lose their position in various ways—for example by failing to attend meetings for six months without good excuse, by being declared bankrupt or through receiving a prison sentence of at least three months.

following year. Thus, for example, those resident at an address on 10 October 1995 are eligible for inclusion under that address on the register which is in force from 16 February 1996 to 15 February 1997. In Northern Ireland there are slightly different requirements.

Generally speaking, those on the electoral register can vote both at parliamentary and local elections, but there are a few people who are qualified to vote in only one kind of election—for example, peers cannot vote at parliamentary elections but can vote (and stand) in local elections. The names of such people are distinguished in the register by a special mark.

Candidates

Most candidates at local government elections stand as representatives of a national political party, although some stand either as independents or as groups representing sectional interests but not aligned with the major national political parties—for example candidates describing themselves as 'ratepayers'. Candidates are now allowed to have their 'description'—in practice often their party affiliation—appear on the ballot paper, although in past years this was not the case.

Candidates must be citizens of Britain, other Commonwealth countries or the Irish Republic, or, from 1996, citizens of the EU, and aged 21 or over. In addition, they must either:

—be registered as local electors in the area of the relevant local authority; or

—have occupied (as owner or tenant) land or premises in that area during the whole of the preceding 12 months; or

—have had their main place of work in the area throughout this 12-month period.

No one may be elected to a council of which he or she is an employee. The Local Government and Housing Act 1989 introduced some further restrictions. Those occupying certain designated senior council jobs or earning more than a certain level are debarred from standing for any council. These restrictions, introduced because of a perceived lack of impartiality where one individual was a councillor in one local authority and a senior official in a nearby council, stemmed from the recommendations of the 1986 Widdicombe Report (see Further Reading). In local government circles, therefore, such posts are popularly referred to as being 'Widdicombed'.

There are also a number of statutory disqualifications designed to ensure that unsuitable people do not stand for election. These include:

—undischarged bankrupts;

—people convicted of illegal or corrupt election practices; and

—people who, within the five years preceding the election date, have been sentenced to more than three months' imprisonment.

A person's eligibility to sit as a councillor can be challenged in the courts by an election petition, but a council has no power to expel one of its members.

Each candidate must be nominated by two electors as proposer and seconder and, except in parish or community council elections, eight other electors for the area must assent to the nomination. Unlike at parliamentary elections, a candidate does not pay a deposit. There is, however, a statutory limit on candidates' election expenses, which at March 1995 was set at £205 plus 4 pence per elector in the ward. Thus, for a ward of 10,000 electors the total allowable expense for each candidate would be £605. All candidates, successful or not, have to make returns of election expenses to the authority for which the election has been held within 35 days of the result being declared.

All candidates for district council elections in Northern Ireland are required to make a declaration against terrorism.

Electoral Divisions and Procedure

Counties in England are divided into electoral divisions, each returning one councillor. Districts in England and Northern Ireland are divided into wards, returning one councillor or more. In Wales and Scotland the electoral areas in the new councils are called electoral divisions and wards respectively. Parishes (in England) and communities (in Wales) may be divided into wards. Wards return at least one councillor, but usually more than one. Depending on the schedule for elections for the particular council (see p. 35), these may be elected all at the same time or sequentially in different years.

The procedure for local government voting in Great Britain is broadly similar to that for parliamentary elections. Voting takes place by secret ballot under the supervision of a presiding officer at polling stations arranged by the returning officer, who is an official of the local authority concerned. One difference is that the polls are open for a slightly shorter period in the day, normally from 08.00 hours to 21.00 hours.[16] Electors must normally vote in person. However, voting by post, or in certain cases by proxy, may be

[16] In a parliamentary election, the polls are open from 07.00 hours to 22.00 hours—see *Parliamentary Elections* (Aspects of Britain: HMSO, 1995).

allowed if a voter cannot attend in person and has properly applied for a postal or proxy vote.

In Great Britain voting is by the 'first past the post' system, with the elector being able to vote for only one candidate if there is only one vacancy. The candidate who receives the greatest number of votes is elected. In the case of, say, three vacancies to be filled in a single ward, electors can vote for up to three candidates, with the three highest being elected. In practice in these circumstances, most electors give all their votes to the three candidates of one chosen party, but a significant proportion distribute their votes between candidates of more than one party, while if, for example, a single independent candidate stands and attracts votes, this will also tend to cause people to split their vote.

In Northern Ireland local government elections are held using proportional representation, and electoral wards are grouped into district electoral areas. The single transferable vote system is used for this. Electors mark the ballot paper in the numbered order of preference, putting '1' against their first choice candidate and so on. At the count, if a candidate is declared elected,[17] surplus votes can then be redistributed to lower preference candidates. Likewise, if a candidate is eliminated, all votes are redistributed.

Newly-elected councillors are required to make a formal acceptance of office, declaring that they will adhere to the national code of conduct for councillors. Failure to do this within 28 days makes their election void.

---

[17] In a single transferable vote count, candidates are elected if their votes exceed the 'quota', the minimum necessary to ensure election. Once all redistribution of surplus votes caused by candidates reaching quota has taken place, the lowest candidate is eliminated and his or her votes redistributed, and so on until all places are filled.

Councillors

Both councillors and senior officers have important roles within the local government system, but the roles are distinct and separate.

The key role of councillors is to decide the overall policy of the council, while the officers are responsible for implementation. The things that councillors might typically decide include:

— the level of the council budget and its distribution between the many different services that the council provides;

— proposed sales of council land;

— whether or not to grant the more controversial planning applications;

— the criteria according to which people's housing applications are assessed;

— the appointment of senior officers; and

— alterations to the council's overall organisation.

A scheme of delegation is necessary to lay down which matters can be decided by officers and do not need to be approved by councillors. Typically the more routine or minor questions are delegated in this way, including operational matters such as deciding to whom to allot a vacant council home, as well as dealing with uncontroversial applications for planning permission or entertainment licensing.

Individual councillors have no power to issue formal instructions to council officers; this can only be done through a properly constituted meeting of the council or one of its committees. However, in practice senior officers work closely with the leader of the council and the chairmen of its committees, since their political influence will normally ensure that their policies would be backed by the council or committee.

Allowances

The post of councillor has always been a form of unpaid service to the community; it is therefore unsalaried. Councillors are, however, paid a basic allowance and may also be entitled to additional allowances and expenses for attending meetings or taking on special responsibilities, such as serving as committee chairmen. Following changes made in April 1995, local authorities are free to decide both the overall amount they wish to spend on allowances and the amounts to be paid to individual councillors. Authorities must publish details of their scheme of allowances and the amounts claimed by each member.

In addition, councils will often provide other assistance to their councillors to help them perform their duties; this might include making typing facilities available or providing them with free stationery and stamps to reply to constituents' letters.

Parish and community councillors cannot claim allowances for duties undertaken within their own council areas. In Scotland community councillors are not eligible for any form of allowance.

Political Organisation

Where a single political party holds a majority of the seats on a council, it clearly controls that council. When no one party holds a majority, the council is said to be under 'no overall control' or 'hung'. In recent years, a large number of councils in Britain have become hung, partly as a result of the Liberal Democrats securing significant representation on councils that might once have had only Labour and Conservative councillors. Various different arrangements are often made to expedite business in these cases. Sometimes two parties that between them command a majority will combine in a pact, while sometimes the largest single party will attempt to carry on a minority administration.

Councillors elected under a particular political banner will normally act as a group. These party groups have long existed informally, but the Local Government and Housing Act 1989 gave them a formally recognised role by allowing two or more councillors to form a political group; committee places are distributed between the groups proportional to their respective strengths.

Each group will normally elect its officers, typically a leader, deputy leader and chief whip. Some groups also elect a chairman to preside over internal group meetings, while other groups give this role to the leader. The leader of the group controlling the council, if there is one, becomes leader of the council. In some councils, the controlling group decides whom to put forward to be elected as mayor or other presiding officer at the annual meeting of the council; in other councils the mayoralty by tradition alternates among the political groups.

Party groups will normally meet ahead of council meetings to go through the agenda and decide on a common line to take on each item. The group's councillors are then all expected to vote in the agreed fashion; those who 'break the whip' may be disciplined in some fashion, for example by suspension from the group. Likewise, a party group's nominees on a specific committee will normally meet ahead of that committee to agree their approach.

The councillors elect annually one of their number to act as the civic head of the authority. This is done at the 'annual meeting' of the council.[18] In many councils, the chosen councillor is known as the mayor, although in district councils without borough status (see p. 24) the title of chairman is generally used instead. Some Scottish councils use the old title of provost; others have 'convenors'. In some cities, as an honorific, the title of lord mayor or lord provost is used. Mayors are ceremonial officers and do not have executive authority, unlike those in most other countries. Mayors have an important ceremonial role, often presiding over functions such as the opening of new council facilities, an annual civic service, council-organised Christmas parties for elderly people and sports competitions held between the schools in the area. As such, they often receive much publicity in local newspapers.

Legal Requirements

Councils are required to act within the framework of the law. Councillors must therefore take care that what they propose would not take the council outside the framework of the law. In this, they receive advice from the council's legal officers. If the council suffers a financial loss as a result of taking an unlawful action, then the district auditor (see p. 73) can take steps to surcharge the councillors responsible and debar them from office. This power is rarely used but when it is, the cases attract considerable attention.

A councillor who has a financial interest in any matter coming before the council must disclose this interest and, unless he or she has received a special dispensation from the Government, may not vote or take part in discussion on it. If this rule is not observed, the councillor may be fined up to £1,000 for each offence. There is,

[18] Councils must hold an 'annual meeting' of the full council to elect a mayor or other presiding officer; the frequency of other full council meetings is at each council's discretion.

however, a general dispensation to allow councillors who are council tenants to vote on setting council rents. A register of councillors' interests is also kept by each council; there is a legal obligation on councillors to make the necessary returns to the council.

Ward Duties

In addition to their responsibilities deciding policy at the town hall, local councillors are also expected to take an interest in very local matters. These problems might be something that affects a number of people, for example traffic congestion in a particular road, or it might be an individual problem. Councillors generally hold 'surgeries'—sessions at set times when constituents can approach them for advice and assistance. They may well also receive a large postbag, particularly if there is, for example, a controversial planning application in the ward.

The sorts of individual problems that councillors get asked to help with are extremely varied, but requests might include assistance with:

—getting council housing repaired;

—sorting out administrative problems over council tax bills or housing benefit payments; or

—finding new council accommodation where the constituent's existing house is overcrowded.

The majority of such requests for assistance cover housing matters. Because councillors have no individual power to instruct council officers (see p. 41), their intervention in such cases has no formal status. In practice, however, officers will usually take seriously their involvement, and the intervention of a councillor can often therefore be helpful in getting a problem resolved.

Administration and Finance

Local Authorities' Powers

Local authorities derive their power from legislation. They can only act under powers conferred by Acts of Parliament. If these powers are exceeded, the local authority concerned is acting, in the legal phrase, *ultra vires* (beyond its power). This is unlawful and can be challenged in a court of law.

Local authorities' functions are far-reaching. Some are mandatory, which means that the authority must do what is required by law; others are purely permissive, allowing an authority to provide services if it wishes. Examples of mandatory duties, services and roles that the relevant tier of local government must provide in its area include:

—acting as an education authority (see p. 28);

—acting as a planning authority (see p. 31);

—providing housing to homeless people in priority need (see p. 29);

—for social services authorities, providing a child protection service to children at risk and a community care package for those who need it; and

—providing a comprehensive library service.

However, local authorities have considerable discretion in deciding what level of provision is required to meet some of these duties.

Expenditure by local authorities is normally limited to the exercise of functions conferred on them by Parliament. Although local authorities are responsible for administering certain services, ministers have powers in some areas to secure a degree of uniformity in standards to safeguard public health or to protect the rights of individual citizens.

Legal Challenge

Because local authorities have to act in accordance with the requirements of the law, it is possible for them to have their decisions challenged in court by the procedure known as 'judicial review'. In such a case, the judge examines how the decision was arrived at, and may order the authority to re-examine the matter if the decision-making process was not properly carried out. The court cannot simply substitute its decision for that of the council.

A large body of case law has grown up as a result of court challenges in the past, which sets precedent to guide councils in future decision-making. For example, there is a requirement for local authorities to act reasonably. The test that is applied is known as 'Wednesbury reasonableness', after a famous court case involving the former Wednesbury borough council. This would be applied not only by the courts, should a case arise concerning the reasonableness of a particular action, but also by local authority lawyers in advising their councillors before a decision is made.

Relations with Central Government

The main link between local authorities and central government in England is the Department of the Environment. It is responsible for policy in a number of areas of great importance for local government, including:

—the general supervision of local government;

—local government finance;

—housing;

—planning; and

—urban regeneration.

In the rest of Britain the local authorities deal with The Scottish Office, the Welsh Office or the Department of the Environment for Northern Ireland, as appropriate. However, other government departments are concerned with one or more local government functions, including education (the Department for Education and Employment), personal social services (the Department of Health), transport (the Department of Transport), police and fire services and electoral matters (the Home Office), and matters relating to certain state benefits which are paid for by central government but administered by local authorities (the Department of Social Security).

The main conduit for discussion between the Government and local government is through the local authority associations. Prior to local government reorganisation, the main ones included:

—the Association of County Councils;

—the Association of District Councils;

—the Association of Metropolitan Authorities;

—the Association of London Government;

—the Convention of Scottish Local Authorities;

—the Committee of Welsh District Councils;

—the Welsh Counties Committee; and

—the Association of Local Authorities of Northern Ireland.

The National Association of Local Councils represents about 7,500 of the parish, town and community councils in England and Wales. It is structured as a federation of 48 county associations.

The Government influences local government programmes by providing advice, paying specific grant or subsidy, approving programmes under certain legislation and controlling capital investment. It can also fix upper limits to the level of council tax levied if it thinks that an authority's spending is excessive (see p. 66).

Central departments consider submissions by local authorities where ministerial consent is required—for example, for certain development plans and by-laws requiring confirmation. Police and fire services are subject to inspection by central government.

International Local Government Organisations and Links

As the importance of the EU to local authorities has grown, particularly as a source of funds, so the need for local government to make its voice heard at an international level has grown. Two international organisations concerned with local government, the International Union of Local Authorities (IULA) and the Council of European Municipalities and Regions (CEMR), include all Britain's local authorities in their membership. In 1990 the two bodies were amalgamated at the European level when the CEMR became the European regional section of the worldwide IULA. The CEMR operates a liaison bureau in Brussels.

International Union of Local Authorities

Founded in Ghent (Belgium) in 1913, the IULA aims to:

—promote the welfare of citizens through more effective local government;

—raise standards of local administration and services;

—encourage the international exchange of information and personal contacts among its members; and

—foster involvement in local government affairs.

The IULA's membership comprises local authority associations and individual local authorities in over 70 countries. Special categories of membership are available to central and regional government ministries, education and research institutes, and also to individuals actively involved in local government or in teaching and research.

The IULA promotes its aims through a varied programme of activities. These include world congresses held every two years, which bring together some 1,000 to 1,500 people from most of the countries with IULA connections. There are also regional seminars and conferences and specialist meetings. A number of training courses are run each year to enable senior local government officials from developing countries to examine a particular subject on a comparative basis through a programme of lectures and study visits in at least three, usually European, countries. Many of the participants are sponsored by the international technical co-operation programmes of the United Nations and other intergovernmental organisations, and further assistance is provided by the governments and local authorities of the host countries. The IULA publishes a monthly newsletter, *Local Government*, and a six-monthly journal, *Planning and Administration*, and its list of publications includes over 150 titles on various aspects of local government.

Council of European Municipalities and Regions (Conseil des Communes d'Europe)

The Council of European Municipalities and Regions seeks to:

—secure, strengthen and protect the autonomy of local authorities;

—develop the European spirit among local and regional communities and authorities with a view to promoting European unity; and

—provide for the participation and representation of local and regional communities and authorities in the European and international institutions.

The CEMR's activities include biennial congresses in different centres, bringing together some 2,500 to 3,000 local elected members and officials, and special conferences and meetings on relevant European themes, often in conjunction with the IULA and in collaboration with EU institutions.

Local Government International Bureau

The British sections of IULA and CEMR operate through the Local Government International Bureau (LGIB), constituted by the British local authority associations. They have closely linked constitutions and their governing bodies usually meet on a joint basis.

The LGIB operates a monitoring service, providing advice and guidance to local authorities on EU developments likely to affect local government interests or services; and participes in CEMR bodies established for the purpose of consultations with EU institutions of behalf of local government. The LGIB also organises British participation in the Council of Europe's Standing Conference of Local and Regional Authorities of Europe, and in IULA and CEMR congresses, conferences and training courses.

The LGIB organises its own conferences and seminars on topics of importance to the EU or beyond. In addition, it advises local authorities and twinning associations on the establishment and operation of twinning links with communities in other countries. It also seeks to facilitate British involvement in the exchange of information, ideas and practices among local and regional authorities in Europe and worldwide; and assists British participation in initiatives to promote and assist the practice of effective local self-government throughout the world, notably in the developing countries. The Bureau is involved in co-ordinating the British local government response to developments in Eastern Europe, including schemes for technical co-operation between British local authorities and their Eastern European counterparts; these are financed by the Foreign & Commonwealth Office.

Committee of the Regions

The EU Committee of the Regions was established under the Maastricht Treaty to advise the European Commission on the regional implications of Community legislation. Britain has 24 representatives, chosen from serving councillors.

Town Twinning

International links are fostered through the process of 'town twinning'. Civic links are established between a local authority in Britain and another overseas—for example, the city of Oxford is twinned with Bonn in Germany, Grenoble in France, Leiden in the

Netherlands and Leon in Nicaragua. This is arranged through the LGIB, which acts as a central clearing house for twinning requests. Sometimes, place-names provide an obvious link—for example Margate in Kent is twinned with Margate, New Jersey in the United States, and Norfolk County Council with Norfolk, Virginia. Visits and hospitality are exchanged between twinned areas on a regular basis.

Citizen's Charter and Charter Marks

Local government has been heavily involved in the Government's Citizen's Charter initiative and the Charter Mark scheme. The aim of the Charter, which was launched in 1991, is to raise the standard of public services and make them more responsive to their users. The Charter sets out a number of principles which the users of public services are entitled to expect, including:

—standards;

—information and openness;

—choice and consultation; and

—courtesy and helpfulness.

The Charter Mark scheme has been introduced to reward excellence in delivering public service. Local authorities have gained a high proportion of Charter Mark awards; of the 1995 awards, 84 out of 224 went to local authorities. Some of the awards have gone to areas which have traditionally attracted many of the complaints—four taxation and benefits offices were among the 1994 Charter Mark winners, compared with none in 1993.

Several local authorities have produced their own Charters setting out the services local residents can expect, as have other related bodies. For example, the London Pensions Fund Authority, which handles pensions for ex-LCC and GLC staff among others, has produced a Charter for its pensioners, including a straightforward complaints procedure, and was awarded the Charter Mark in 1994.

Committees

A local authority does relatively little of its member-level business in full council. Most is instead done in committee. It is up to each council to decide what committees to set up and what their terms of reference will be. The differing responsibilities of the different types of council will influence this very much. For example, an English non-metropolitan district council does not have social services responsibilities, so would not need a social services committee. However, housing is one of its key functions and so it would almost certainly have a housing committee. A London borough is responsible for both, and so would usually have both committees—although at least one borough has chosen to set up a single housing and social services committee responsible for both matters.

An alternative approach is that of 'decentralisation', in which the local authority is divided into neighbourhoods and typically one committee for each neighbourhood is set up consisting of all the councillors from that part of the borough. These committees then take decisions on a wide range of different issues concerning that area. This approach was adopted, for example, by the London Borough of Tower Hamlets between 1986 and 1994. However, following a change of political control in the 1994 local elections, a more traditional committee structure was reinstated there.

In England and Wales committees generally have to reflect the political composition of the council (although the legislation governing this specifically excludes parish or community councils). In practice, this is often also the case in Scotland, although it is not enforced by legislation. People who are not members of the council may be co-opted onto decision-making committees and can speak and take part in debates; they cannot normally vote.

Public Access

The public (including the press) are admitted to council, committee and sub-committee meetings, and have access to agendas, reports and minutes of meetings and certain background papers. Local authorities may exclude the public from meetings and withhold these papers only in limited circumstances. For example, where the council is discussing the sale of land, it will be necessary to keep the size of the bids confidential, as otherwise the highest bidder might reduce the size of bid so as to be only just above the next highest. Likewise, in the relatively rare cases that councillors make decisions that affect individual named members of staff, there are obviously good grounds for confidentiality. Cases such as these can therefore be treated as confidential.

Under the local government legislation, there is certain business that councillors must treat as confidential, while for most categories of 'closed' business the councillors have discretion whether or not to deal with it in closed session. Confidential reports, minutes and agendas are often printed on paper of a different colour so that councillors can easily distinguish them from ordinary business.

The views of the public have to be sought by councils when drawing up development plans (see p. 32). It is also common for councils to seek the public's views on many other areas of local authority services as well. This can be done in a variety of ways, for example by the council organising consultation meetings or by sending out questionnaires.

Many councils have provision in their standing orders (see below) for members of the public to come to council or committee meetings as a deputation and address the councillors for a short time. Petitions are also often addressed to councillors, for example calling on the council to improve its services in some way or not to proceed with the proposed closure of a particular facility.

Standing Orders

A council regulates its business through its standing orders. Some of these are determined at national level; for example, matters such as the right of individual councillors to have the way they voted on a particular question recorded in the minutes are a requirement of law. In other areas, the council has discretion to make its own arrangements. Standing orders might typically include:

—arrangements for summoning council and committee meetings and the notice periods that must be given;

—quorums at meetings;

—provisions as to what business is reserved for full council;

—stipulations regarding the length of time that speeches at meetings can last;

—provisions concerning the taking of minutes; and

—powers for the chairman to take action against disorderly conduct.

Finance

Local authorities account for around one-quarter of all public expenditure in Britain (see Table 3). The Government is therefore concerned not just with the level of spending on particular services but with authorities' overall level of expenditure, borrowing and taxation. Their current expenditure affects the level of taxation and the balance between the public and private sectors, with implications for economic growth and the level of inflation. Local authority borrowing affects the public sector borrowing requirement, the rate of monetary growth and interest rates. Local authorities are required to balance their revenue budgets; budgeting for a deficit is not permitted.

Table 3: Local Authority Expenditure in General Government Expenditure

	1984–85	1985–86	1986–87	1987–88
Local authority contribution to general government expenditure (£ million)	38,935	39,801	42,187	45,317
Local authority share of general government expenditure (per cent)	25.5	24.7	24.9	25.4

Table 3: Local Authority Expenditure in General Government Expenditure *(contd.)*

	1988–89	1989–90	1990–91	1991–92
Local authority contribution to general government expenditure (£ million)	47,006	53,538	57,517	64,257
Local authority share of general government expenditure (per cent)	25.2	26.1	25.7	26.3

	1992–93	1993–94[a]
Local authority contribution to general government expenditure (£ million)	68,760	69,038
Local authority share of general government expenditure (per cent)	25.6	24.5

Source: *Office for National Statistics.*

[a] Provisional figures.

Authorities in England, Scotland and Wales have four main sources of revenue:

—government grant;

—local taxation levied on residents, now in the form of the council tax;

—the national non-domestic rate; and

—fees and charges.

Table 4 shows how the source of expenditure has varied over time between government grant, local taxation on residents and non-domestic rates. It excludes spending financed by fees and charges.

Table 4: Funding of Revenue Expenditure, England

Year	Source of funds (%)		
	Government grant	Non-domestic rates	Domestic rates/ community charge/ council tax
1981–82	56	25	20
1989–90	44	29	26
1990–91[a]	42	29	28
1991–92	53	31	16
1992–93	55	29	17
1993–94[bc]	55	27	16
1994–95[d]	57	24	17

Source: *Local Government Financial Statistics England 1990/91–1993/94.*

[a] First year of community charge.
[b] First year of council tax.
[c] Estimated outturn.
[d] Budgeted figures.

Government Grant

There are two types of government grant—that specifically made to certain services such as education and the police, and a more general revenue support grant not linked to a particular service.

The revenue support grant is distributed to authorities on the basis of a standard spending assessment (SSA). This calculates for each authority the level of expenditure it would be appropriate for it to incur in order to provide the services for which it is responsible to a standard level, taking account of the area's characteristics and the Government's public expenditure plans. An authority's aggregate SSA is calculated on the basis of the services it provides, using formulae for each service. In general terms, these formulae multiply a unit cost by the population or, where more appropriate, the users (such as the number of school pupils). Unit costs take account of factors which vary the need for local authority expenditure, such as economic deprivation. Revenue support grant is distributed to each authority by reference to its SSA such that, if all authorities budgeted at the level of their SSA, council taxes would be broadly similar across the country.

In other areas, the Government supports local authority expenditure directly. For example, local authorities are responsible for the administration of housing benefit and council tax benefit. Claims for these benefits are normally received by the local authority—either directly or forwarded by the Department of Social Security—and it is then responsible for assessing the claims according to the relevant regulations and for paying the benefits. The Government largely reimburses councils for these payments.

The Government also sometimes makes financial help available to local authorities to help them meet the costs of dealing with unexpected emergencies. The so-called 'Bellwin' scheme was used twice in 1994 to help local authorities meet the costs of flooding and landslips following severe storms.

The Government has sought to contain the overall level of local government expenditure for a number of years, dating back to the mid-1970s, when the then Secretary of State for the Environment warned local authorities in a phrase that has become famous in local government circles—'the party's over'. Reductions in grant to penalise overspending authorities were one means of attempting this before the introduction of rate capping in 1984 (see p. 66), and this partly underlies the reduction in the share of spending coming from central government grant during the 1980s shown in Table 4.

Local Taxation on Residents

Local government taxation in Great Britain has been the subject of two major reforms in recent years; firstly in 1989 and 1990 the old 'rating' system was replaced by the community charge for residents of domestic property and the national non-domestic rate (NNDR) levied on other properties. Subsequently in 1993 the community charge was replaced by the council tax, which is levied on domestic property.

Rates

The rates were a property tax which went back centuries—parish relief in the 18th century had been paid for by a rate. Each property had its rateable value assessed, which was the notional amount that it could be rented out for. The local council then decided its budget, and hence its need for money from the rates. From this the 'poundage'—the percentage of the rateable value to be levied as a rate—was set.

Under the old system, where each local authority set its own poundage, some businesses faced a poundage more than three times higher than others, which distorted competition. The ability for rates bills to rise steeply with little warning also made it difficult for businesses to plan ahead. These problems led to a decision to replace the rating system in Great Britain. In Northern Ireland, the rating system still remains, with a district rate set by each district and a uniform regional rate throughout Northern Ireland levied by the Northern Ireland Office.

Community Charge

The community charge—commonly known as the 'poll tax'—was introduced in Scotland in April 1989 under the Abolition of Domestic Rates etc. (Scotland) Act 1987 and in England and Wales in April 1990 under the Local Government Finance Act 1988. All adults were liable to pay, with a few exceptions such as the severely mentally impaired. Students at recognised educational establishments paid a reduced community charge, at one-fifth of the normal rate. A register was set up to record liability to the community charge; this was separate from the electoral register.

A flat rate tax was set by each council concerned, which was calculated by dividing the requirement for revenue to be raised from the community charge by the number of people on the register, after making allowances for the anticipated level of non-payment. However, the less well-off were entitled to help, which meant that up to 80 per cent of the cost could be met by central government in the form of community charge benefit. About a quarter of chargepayers benefited from such reductions. Reductions were also available to about half of all community chargepayers under a scheme which provided assistance where the change from the former domestic rating system to the community charge would otherwise have resulted in significant increases in payments.

The community charge was not well received by the public. Many people felt that its flat rate nature was unfair and penalised households with large numbers of adults. The fact that the charge was levied on people rather than property also made it harder to collect. An attempt was made to redress this in the 1991 Budget, when the rate of value-added tax was increased by 2.5 per cent, to 17.5 per cent. The proceeds were used to increase central government grant to local authorities so as to reduce all community charges by £140. The effects of this are also reflected in Table 3. However, the community charge remained unpopular, and the decision was therefore taken to revert to a property-based system for domestic taxation—the council tax.

Council Tax

The council tax was introduced by the Local Government Finance Act 1992 and came into operation in April 1993. The non-domestic rating system was unaffected by this change.

The council tax is a property-related tax payable by the resident(s) of a dwelling. Every dwelling has been assigned to one of eight valuation bands on the basis of its estimated sale price on 1 April 1991. This exercise was carried out by the Valuation Office, an agency of the Inland Revenue. There are separate banding structures for England, Wales and Scotland. In England the lowest band, Band A, is for those dwellings worth less than £40,000, and the highest, Band H, for dwellings worth £320,000 or more. Each band has a multiplier which is set in reference to Band D (see Table 5). The multiplier limits the difference in levels of council tax between the bands. The multipliers are the same in Wales and Scotland. Any householder who was unhappy with the band into which his or her property was placed had an initial right of appeal to an independent tribunal. By the end of September 1995 nearly 99 per cent of the 864,000 appeals received had been settled.

Table 5: Dwellings by Council Tax Banding in England, 1994

Band	Value	Multiplier	Number of dwellings ('000)
A	Up to £40,000	6/9	5,309
B	£40,001–£52,000	7/9	3,879
C	£52,001–£68,000	8/9	4,406
D	£68,001–£88,000	9/9	2,945
E	£88,001–£120,000	11/9	1,821
F	£120,001–£160,000	13/9	975
G	£160,001–£320,000	15/9	740
H	£320,000+	18/9	118

Source: Inland Revenue Valuation Office.

Table 6: Council Tax Banding in Scotland and Wales

Band	Scotland, value	Wales, value
A	Up to £26,999	Up to £29,999
B	£27,000–£34,999	£30,000–£38,999
C	£35,000–£44,999	£39,000–£50,999
D	£45,000–£57,999	£51,000–£65,999
E	£58,000–££79,999	£66,000–£89,999
F	£80,000–£105,999	£90,000–£119,999
G	£106,000–£211,999	£120,000–£239,999
H	£212,000+	£240,000+

Source: *Local Government Finance Act 1992.*

The basic council tax bill assumes at least two adults resident in the dwelling. However, reductions apply in some cases:

— where there are fewer than two residents, the bill will be discounted by 25 per cent when there is only one resident and by 50 per cent if there are no residents;

— in certain circumstances, dwellings will be exempt from council tax;

— for those on low incomes, council tax benefit is available to help them meet up to their full liability; and

— a transitional relief scheme has helped to ensure that no one faces an unreasonably large increase in the bill as a direct result of the change from the community charge to the council tax.

Since the introduction of the council tax in 1993–94, both tiers of local government have each received revenue support grant and non-domestic rate income from central government to support their spending. Each authority sets its own council tax. All council tax income is paid into the collection fund. The collection fund is administered by the billing authority, which collects all council taxes. Parish spending is included in the district's demand on the collection fund.

The average council tax in 1995–96 for a two-adult Band C property is £543 before transitional relief, up 5.3 per cent on 1994–95. The relevant local authorities are responsible for sending out a bill and collecting payment. Taxpayers can opt to spread the payments over the year in up to ten instalments. The council tax has been widely accepted as fair. This has been reflected in local authorities steadily improving their collection rates. In England in the first year of council tax there was an 8 per cent increase in collection rates over the community charge, followed by a further increase in 1994–95. There has, however, been a considerable variation in collection rates between local authorities.

Capping

The Government's policy in the early to mid-1980s of reducing grants to high-spending councils sometimes led not to a reduction in spending as intended, but to large increases in the rates. These increases led the Government to introduce a system of 'rate capping' under the Rates Act 1984. These powers have continued under the subsequent reforms, so that there is now a system of 'council tax capping'.

The 'cap' is technically not a limit on the level of the council tax, but rather on the level of an authority's budget. Thus, all councils, whether or not they collect council tax directly, are subject to these limits. Since a local authority's income from government grants and the NNDR is fixed before the start of the financial year, the effect of controlling the overall size of the budget is also to control the level of council tax, since that is the other major source of income. Provisional cap levels are announced by the Government in advance of the budget-making process, so that authorities have an indication of the likely level above which their budget might be capped.

Most councils set a budget within the levels the Government has announced. In 1995–96, the Government designated ten councils in England for capping, using criteria examining the proposed size of increase and the level of the resulting budget relative to SSA. Once an authority has been designated and a cap proposed, it has 28 days either to challenge or accept the proposed cap. Nine of the ten English authorities designated in 1995–96 challenged their cap; of these, three were allowed full or partial relaxations of the proposed cap.

Non-Domestic Rates

Most industrial and commercial property, with the exception of that used for agriculture and forestry, is subject to a non-domestic rate. Each property has a rateable value which broadly represents its annual rental value in the open market. For every pound of rateable value, 43.2 pence is paid as business rate in the financial year 1995–96, less any relevant adjustments. So, if a property has a rateable value of £20,000, the amount paid is £20,000 multiplied by 0.432 (the multiplier for 1995–96), which equals £8,640. To help those facing large increases in their rateable values as a result of the 1990 and 1995 revaluations, the Government introduced a transitional scheme to limit increases in bills. For 1995–96, increases as a result of the revaluation were limited to 10 per cent in real terms— 7.5 per cent for small properties. The Exchequer contributed over £500 million towards the cost of the scheme in England in 1995–96. The rest of the cost was met by limiting reductions in the bills of those whose rateable value fell significantly as a result of the revaluation.

Annual increases in the multiplier, which is the same throughout England, are limited by law to the rate of inflation or less. A survey commissioned by the Government found that rates were not a significant burden for most companies, representing only 2 per cent of turnover.

The sum raised by the non-domestic rate is paid into central pools in England and Wales—after the costs of collection were deducted, this came to £9,404 million for England in 1994–95.

Funds from the pools are distributed to local authorities in proportion to their adult population. Further revaluations under the present system will take place at five-year intervals.

Table 7: Total Rateable Values

England, April 1994	£ million
Offices	8,190
Shops	6,749
Factories	4,226
Warehouses	2,789
Other	8,258
Total	30,212

Source: Inland Revenue Valuation Office.

Fees and Charges

Local authorities are under a duty to provide many services free of charge. However, there are certain services and amenities from which local authorities may gain revenue through charging. Examples where charges are normally made include the use of leisure facilities and the provision of refuse collection services to businesses.

Borrowing

Local authorities are allowed to borrow money long term to finance new capital expenditure and also to refinance loans raised for capital finance. Authorities are not permitted to borrow long term to finance revenue expenditure but may borrow short term in anticipation of revenues receivable. Spending on capital projects out of revenue funds is, however, freely allowed. Local authorities have to maintain separate capital accounts to distinguish their capital from their revenue spending.

Most long-term borrowing by authorities is from the Public Works Loan Board, which draws its funds from the Government's National Loans Fund. Authorities may also borrow from financial institutions or by issuing stock or sterling commercial paper upon the London Stock Exchange, by issuing bonds which may or may not be quoted on the Exchange, or by issuing bills. All loan charges are secured against the revenues of the authority and represent a first charge on those revenues.

Capital Expenditure

In April 1990 a new system of capital finance for local authorities was introduced. This controls the amount of capital expenditure which local authorities can finance from borrowing and other credit through the use of credit approvals issued annually by the Government. Capital expenditure may also be financed from capital grants, from revenue funds and from part of the receipts from property sales—the remaining part of these receipts must be set aside to redeem debt. Generally speaking, 75 per cent of the proceeds from housing sales and 50 per cent of the proceeds from non-housing capital disposals must be retained in this way for debt redemption. However, at times the Government has introduced temporary relaxations to these rules—for example, at present local authorities are able to spend a higher proportion of the proceeds of any sales of their interests in public airport companies, car parks, shops and crematoria.

Every year the Government effectively sets limits, through the use of credit approvals, on the overall amount which a local authority may borrow. Subject to these and to their legal powers, authorities have almost complete discretion to spend according to locally determined priorities. The largest item is housing, which in 1994–95 accounted for 34 per cent of gross capital expenditure in England. The Government may, however, allow supplementary credit approvals (SCAs)—in other words, permission for extra borrowing—for specific projects. For example, many urban regeneration projects have been funded by the Government giving SCAs to the local authorities concerned. In 1994–95, net basic credit approvals for English local authorities totalled £1,907 million. SCAs of about £850 million were also issued.

The Budget Process

The setting of the annual council budget is a very major process and takes a good deal of time. This is understandable when one considers that many councils are dealing with very large budgets— perhaps £250 million in the case of a London borough, and much more for some of the larger counties. Therefore, although a budget has to be set in time for the beginning of a new financial year in April, the planning may well have been under way since the previous summer.

A typical process might involve the authority's main committee dealing with the budget—which would usually be called the policy and resources committee—receiving a report from officers in the summer for the budget round. This would lay out what the officers felt the likely overall level of spending the council would be allowed under the Government's capping rules. If this might entail reductions in spending in real terms, the councillors would probably instruct the different chief officers to prepare suggested savings in their respective areas. This might be done for different levels of cuts—for example, the officers might be told to suggest 2 per cent cuts, further savings to bring the level to 4 per cent and maybe higher levels if it was felt likely that cuts of this magnitude might be required.

Following the national Budget Day in the autumn and the associated announcement of the local government finance settlement by central government, the local authority would then know what its overall spending limit was likely to be. A decision would be taken in the policy and resources committee as to the level at which the budget should be set. The committee would then have to decide how spending would be distributed between the different departments, and each committee would then need to determine how to spend its share of the total.

The final budget, derived from the various committee decisions, would then come to the full council to be approved. If the council was one directly responsible for collecting council tax, the budget level would then be fed into the calculations to produce a council tax level. Also needing to be taken into account would be the level of income from government grant and other sources, including the use of existing reserves, the requirements of precepting authorities, the size of the council tax base and the assumed collection rate. Once these figures were available, the council would be in a position to make the formal resolution to set the council tax levels. This has to be done by 11 March each year.

Table 8 shows how local authorities in England divide their spending between different services.

Table 8: Local Authority Expenditure by Service, 1992–93

	Net current expenditure (all local authorities in England) £ million
Education (including school catering)	20,896
Police	5,208
Personal social services and port health	4,973
Local environmental services	4,914
Housing benefit	3,305
Local transport	2,288
Fire	1,116
Other Home Office services[a]	757
Libraries, museums and art galleries	688
Non-HRA housing[b]	324
Employment	175
Consumer protection	127
Agricultural services	28
Total net current expenditure	44,797

Source: *Local Government Financial Statistics England 1990/91–1993/94.*

[a] Includes such areas as probation services and electoral registration.

[b] Certain housing services, such as home improvement grants and relief of homelessness, fall outside the HRA.

Note: The difference between the total and the sum of its component parts is due to rounding.

Once a budget has been set and the new financial year has begun, councillors will monitor the level of spending by receiving regular reports from officers at their committee meetings. It may become necessary to amend the budget to cope with unexpected circumstances—for example a higher than anticipated number of homeless families needing to be housed. To balance this, there may be savings elsewhere—for example, the council may have budgeted a certain sum for legal expenses and awards against it, which as the year progresses may come to look over-pessimistic. In other cases it may be necessary to spend money from reserves or balances in order to stay within the budgeted figure.

Financial Safeguards

Each council must appoint a professionally qualified chief finance officer responsible for drawing up the council's accounts and for warning councillors if the council is likely to face an unlawful deficit on annual expenditure or if it incurs unlawful expenditure. Any report from the chief finance officer must be considered within 21 days.

Local authorities must make their accounts available for public inspection during the audit process, and must advertise this.

Auditors

Local councils' annual accounts must be audited by independent auditors appointed by the Audit Commission in England and Wales, or by the Commission for Local Authority Accounts in Scotland. In Northern Ireland this role is exercised by the chief local government auditor, who is appointed by the Department of the Environment for Northern Ireland.

The Audit Commission appoints auditors either from its own staff or from private accountancy firms. The auditor is required to undertake a financial and regulatory audit and to express an opinion on the accounts. The Commission's code of audit practice, approved by Parliament, prescribes the ways in which the auditor carries out this work. The auditor must also ensure that the local authority has secured value for money in its use of services. In addition, the auditor is required to consider whether to make a report in the public interest on any particular issues which come to notice in the course of the audit.

A local authority's accounts must be made available for public inspection and electors may question the auditor about them or object to any item in them. If the auditor considers any item of expenditure to be illegal, he or she can apply to a court of law for a declaration to that effect. If the court grants the declaration, it may also impose a surcharge on anyone responsible for unlawful expenditure or wilful misconduct unless an action was reasonable or carried out in the belief that the spending was legal.

A councillor surcharged on an amount over £2,000 can be disqualified from membership of a local authority for five years. If the auditor's work reveals a fraudulent transaction, he or she can order the person responsible to repay the money involved. There is a right of appeal to a court against such an order. Auditors are empowered to issue notices stopping authorities from taking action which they consider would result in unlawful expenditure.

An extraordinary audit of an authority's accounts may be required at any time, either by the Government on the grounds of public interest, or by the Commission following an application by a local government elector or as a consequence of an auditor's report.

In addition to the procedures for auditing accounts, each local authority must supply annual financial returns to the Government. These provide an additional safeguard against improper financial activities and a source of national statistics on local government finance. The Audit Commission undertakes comparative and other studies of local authority services, so as to recommend improvements in economy, efficiency and effectiveness. It also has the power to examine the impact of ministerial directions and statutory provisions on value for money in local authority services.

In Scotland the Commission for Local Authority Accounts, an independent body whose chief officer is the Controller of Audit, carries out audits using either its own staff or a private firm. The Controller reports to the Commission on such matters as illegal payments and losses or deficiencies in the accounts of local authorities. The Commission must send such reports, together with their findings, to the Secretary of State for Scotland and may recommend that any person responsible be required to repay a sum up to the amount of the illegal payment, loss or deficiency. The Commission also undertakes value for money studies.

Local Government Complaints System

Local authorities are encouraged to resolve complaints through internal mechanisms, and members of the public will often ask their own councillor for assistance in this. Local authorities must also appoint a monitoring officer whose duties include ensuring that the local authority acts lawfully in the conduct of its business.

Allegations of local government maladministration leading to injustice may be investigated by statutory independent Commissioners for Local Administration, often known as 'local government ombudsmen'. In England the Commission for Local Administration comprises three Local Commissioners, each responsible for a particular area of the country. There is also a similar Commission for Wales with one Commissioner. Some local government activities are excluded from the arrangements, notably commercial, contractual and personnel matters. A report is issued on each complaint subject to a full investigation and, if injustice caused by maladministration is found, the local ombudsman normally suggests a remedy. The council must consider the report and reply to it.

In Scotland there is a Commissioner for Local Administration who investigates allegations of maladministration. The system is broadly similar to that in England and Wales, although certain arrangements vary slightly. In Northern Ireland a Commissioner for Complaints deals with complaints alleging injustices suffered as a result of maladministration by district councils and certain other public bodies.

A review of the local government ombudsman service in England began in July 1995.

Staff

Local authorities in England employ almost 2 million people, including administrative, professional, technical and clerical staff, and teachers. About 45 per cent of staff are part time.

It is against the law for an authority to employ one of its own councillors; this rule is designed to avoid possible conflicts of interest. A few appointments, such as chief education officers, fire officers and directors of social services, must be made by all the authorities responsible for the functions concerned. Each authority must designate one of its officers as 'head of the paid service'; if the authority has a chief executive, he or she would take this role. Councils are otherwise generally responsible within national policy requirements for determining the size, composition and deployment of their workforces.

Table 9: Local Authority Staff in England

Category	Whole-time equivalents, 1995[a]
Education—teaching	372,600
—other	262,000
Construction	63,200
Social services	245,900
Public libraries, museums and art galleries	30,900
Leisure and recreation	62,700
Environmental health	17,600
Refuse, recycling and cleansing	24,800
Housing	67,900
Planning and economic development	25,400
Engineering and technical services	56,500
Corporate services—finance and computing	57,100
—other	64,400
Fire service—regulars and others	39,700
Other services[b]	21,400
Total	1,411,800

Source: Local Authority Joint Staffing Watch.

[a] Excludes staff in grant-maintained schools and in services which have been contracted out following competitive tendering.

[b] Includes staff not included in listed services and agency staff.

Note: The difference between the total and the sum of its component parts is due to rounding.

All local authorities are required to publish staffing figures for individual services annually, based on staffing levels in June. This is designed to help councillors, local residents and officials to consider and compare their own authorities' staffing levels with previous periods and against national trends. Staff costs, such as wages and salaries, account for almost 55 per cent of authorities' net current expenditure.

Appointment

Senior appointments are normally made on the recommendation of the council committee or committees concerned. Posts may be filled either by promotion or transfer of existing staff or after advertisements in newspapers or specialist journals. It is a common practice to appoint a group of committee members to interview candidates and make a selection which may later have to be confirmed by the council as a whole.

Less senior appointments are normally made by the heads of departments in accordance with an establishment laid down by the council. Again, posts will normally be advertised. The method may vary, with more specialised posts probably being advertised in specialist journals—for example, in titles aimed at social workers where it necessary to recruit a qualified social worker—and less specialised jobs in the local press for the area concerned.

Conditions of Employment

Pay and conditions of service for staff are generally settled through negotiations between representatives of employers and trade unions. The largest negotiating bodies are the National Joint Council for Local Authorities' Administrative, Professional, Technical and Clerical Services and the National Joint Council for Local Authorities' Services (Manual Workers). For the great majority of local government officers, the first of these councils is also concerned with matters such as the maintenance of agreed standards of entry to the service and recognition of appropriate qualifying examinations for promotion.

Local authorities have a national statutory contributory pension scheme which all full-time and most part-time employees are eligible to join. Local authority pension funds have an over-all market value of around £47,000 million. There are also contributory pension schemes for the police and fire services. The Department for Education and Employment runs a pension scheme for teachers to which employees and local authority employers contribute.

Pay and conditions for employees of parish and community councils are a matter for agreement between council and employee, although some guidance is given by the National Association of Local Councils.

The main trade union representing local government officers is Unison, which is the largest trade union in Britain. It was formed from a merger of the Confederation of Health Service Employees, the National and Local Government Officers' Association and the National Union of Public Employees. Unison has 1.3 million members, of whom 860,000 work in local government. The general union GMB also represents about 140,000 members in local government, predominantly in manual jobs.

The employers' organisation is the Local Government Management Board.

Code of Conduct

All local government officers are expected to conform to a code of conduct drawn up by the local authority associations and the Local Government Management Board. The code stresses that a local government officer's conduct must be of such a standard as to ensure public confidence in his or her integrity. It states that the officer should not subordinate his or her duty to private interests or put himself or herself in a position where duty and private interests could conflict. Any additional employment undertaken by an officer must not conflict with the authority's interests or in any way weaken public confidence in the conduct of its business.

Professional Bodies

There are a large number of specialist professional bodies to which council officers may belong. Examples of these include the Chartered Institute of Public Finance and Accountancy, the Institute of Trading Standards Administration, the Institute of Burial and Cremation Administration, and the Institution of Environmental Health Officers. These bodies generally seek to raise standards in their respective areas, act as a forum for discussion of matters of interest, and may offer professional qualifications to those who meet their standards.

Appendix 1: Local Government in 1900

An example of the workings of local government in an urban area at the turn of the century can be found in the annual report for the Metropolitan Borough of Camberwell covering the period 1900–01. The borough was a new creation, having been set up under the London Government Act 1899 covering the Camberwell, Dulwich, Nunhead and Peckham districts of south London, now part of the London Borough of Southwark. The Borough of Camberwell replaced the old Camberwell Vestry Board, which was itself set up under the Metropolis Management Act 1855.

Much of the early business concerned the changeover. At the final meeting of the Vestry Board the Chairman, Mr E. R. Phillips, made a speech summing up the achievements of the Vestry during its 45-year existence. In part it showed civic pride in humble but necessary facilities:

'Nowhere could a patriotic Camberwellian get much more of quiet satisfaction than by a visit to our public wash-houses, or a more bracing tonic than by a well-timed visit to our swimming baths. Then to follow these up by a study of our bath records would enhance his gratification. What can be more delightful to a simple-hearted social reformer than to see a week's washing of a workman's family got through with ease—the articles cleaned, dried and mangled and taken home ready for use, and all for 3d.?'[19]

Items of business arising from the transition also included the resignation of the long-serving Vestry Accountant, whose workload would have been greatly increased by the change. He took advantage of the compensation available for those who lost their jobs through the change. Other important questions also arose from the change:

[19] 3d in pre-decimal currency is slightly more than 1p today.

'The Committee deemed it desirable to apply for a Royal Grant of Arms to the Borough of Camberwell... in accordance with the resolution of the Borough Council, the Town Clerk placed himself in communication with the College of Heralds. Some difficulty was achieved in making the Borough Arms sufficiently indicative, and at the same time presenting a coat which would not be too heavily charged. The one ultimately agreed upon is, it is believed, the best that could have been made under the circumstances.'

The resulting coat of arms is still to be seen in the area to this day, for example adorning some municipal housing projects.

The new council was welcomed into the fold of local authorities:

'A letter was considered from the Association of Municipal Corporations cordially inviting the Borough of Camberwell to become a member of the Association... the annual subscription... is based on the number of inhabitants in the Borough, and the amount of subscription from the Borough of Camberwell, as it contains more than 200,000 inhabitants,[20] would be fifteen guineas[21] per annum... The Council decided to become a member of the Association, and appointed The Worshipful the Mayor and the Town Clerk as its delegates.'

The new council set up several committees, not all of which would be familiar today:

— the Finance Committee, with the Rating Sub-committee, the Law and Parliamentary Sub-committee, the New Streets Sub-committee and the Accounts Sub-committee;

— the Works Committee, with the Roads Sub-committee and the Works and Depots Sub-committee;

[20] Today's London Borough of Southwark, covering a much larger area, has no more than roughly 230,000 people, an indication of how much more densely populated central London was at the turn of the century.
[21] Fifteen guineas is equivalent to £15.75.

— the Public Health Committee, with the Baths and Underground Conveniences Sub-committee, the Cemetery and Mortuary Sub-committee and the Combined Drainage and Works Sub-committee;

— the Libraries Committee;

— the Assessment Committee; and

— the Charities Committee.

To take just one example, the Baths and Underground Conveniences Sub-committee had the following terms of reference:

'To deal with all questions arising under the Baths and Wash-houses Act, 1846, and the Amending Acts; to consider and investigate all matters connected with the underground conveniences and report; to confer with representatives from the Libraries Committee upon the subject of the buildings proposed to be erected upon the Wells Street site, and all other matters connected with the site and report; and to examine and report upon all Bills relating to the Baths and Underground Conveniences.'

The Wells Street (now Wells Way) site was indeed developed as a library and wash-house. The building still belongs to the London Borough of Southwark, no longer used for its original purposes but for other community uses.

Overcrowded dwellings were a major concern. The Public Health Committee reports that:

'It was decided that Sanitary Inspector Kerslake, who had charge of the Hollington Street area, should deal only with the question of overcrowding in that district, and for that purpose should make inspections at night-time.

The following is a short summary of Inspector Kerslake's report on the subject of overcrowding in the area mentioned:—

"I may say there has been a decided improvement since 1897 in Hollington and Sultan Streets, that the overcrowding has decreased, and also that the one and two-roomed tenements have materially decreased. . . in my opinion this improvement may be attributed to the working of the By-Laws as to Houses Let in Lodgings." '

However, by the time of the 1901–02 annual report, stronger measures were being called for. The newly-established Housing of the Working Classes Committee reported:

'One of the first matters to engross the attention of the Committee was the absolute necessity for grappling with the housing question in the Hollington Street area. A sub-committee... was appointed to inspect certain property in this neighbourhood then upon the market. As a result of their inspection, the Committee felt justified in recommending the Council to acquire the leases of seventeen houses in Beckett Street, eleven in Toulon Street, four in Sultan Street and four in Hollington Street, in order to give the council a controlling interest in this district. This recommendation was adopted by the Council and the leasehold interests in the thirty-six houses referred to were acquired by the Borough for the sum of £3,920.'

The streets concerned have long since vanished, the area having been redeveloped as blocks of flats.

Before its demise, the Vestry was concerned about the supply of burial land. It was feared that space in what is now called Camberwell Old Cemetery would run short. An opportunity to correct this came with the offer of land near Honor Oak:

'The Vestry decided to purchase the 30 acres for £16,500, and the additional 2½ acres for £3,000... opposition was also encountered from the Borough Council of Lewisham and a certain number of residents in the vicinity of the proposed new cemetery.'

In the event, what is now Camberwell New Cemetery was not laid out until after the First World War. Not all the original purchase had been needed as a cemetery in the 1920s, so part of the land was used as a recreation ground pending its eventual need for burials. However, in an echo of earlier disagreements, controversy arose again in the 1990s as burial land in the new cemetery ran short. Southwark Council decided to take some of the recreation area land into the cemetery, a proposal opposed by many local residents and the London Borough of Lewisham.

The borough's vehicles were, of course, horse-drawn. The 1900–01 report records that the total cost of fodder was £3,652 5s 6d, or an average of 12s 1¼d per horse per week. The report continues:

'The average number of Borough Council's horses for the year for all purposes has been 114... during the year 8 horses were slaughtered or died, and 13 others sold, being considered unfit to be continued for our work.'

The LCC provided the top tier of local government in London at this time. Among its responsibilities was tramways. Camberwell's Works and General Purposes Committee had to consider the LCC's plans for new tram routes:

'A deputation of owners and residents of Denmark Hill, &c., attended, and Mr Percival Nairne addressed the Council and handed in a memorial objecting to the route, and asking the Borough Council to oppose the Bill.'

This was in vain, for the council decided to support the Bill. The Vestry had earlier had a dispute with the LCC after it had repaved the road, including the margin of another LCC tramline, with wooden blocks. This entailed removing the LCC's granite setts which, the LCC claimed, would last longer, be cheaper for it to maintain and would still have some residual value when the time came for them to be replaced. Counsel's opinion was sought and the answer came back that the LCC was entitled to have its stones returned to it or be compensated for their value. London's last tram ran in 1952, but present proposals would see their reappearance in Croydon.

The LCC was also concerned about various nuisances, and had called representatives from Camberwell Vestry and other areas to a conference to consider, among other things:

'regulations for the further suppression of street cries, railway whistles, and other objectionable and unnecessary noises within the county of London.'

To this day, noise is the main source of complaints to environmental health officers.

The LCC was not the only other local government body the borough had to deal with:

'A letter was received from the Correspondent for the East Lambeth Division of the School Board for London with regard to the decision to charge 2d. per head to the pupils of [evening continuation schools] for admission to the second-class swimming baths instead of 1d., as was charged last year, and asking that the matter might be reconsidered. Having regard to the fact that many of these pupils are adults it was decided to adhere to the charge of 2d. for the second-class bath.'

Nor did events in the outside world pass the councillors by. In January 1901, news came of the death of Queen Victoria. The council adjourned as a mark of respect, having first resolved to send an address of condolences to the new King Edward VII. The report proudly notes:

'It may be of interest to record that the Borough Council of Camberwell has been honoured in being the first Metropolitan Borough Council to be received by His Majesty and to have presented its address in person.'

Appendix 2: Changing Views of Local Government

Post-War Britain 1946, the first in the series of annual *Britain* handbooks that COI continues to publish, gives this official view of local government:

'Like almost every other British institution, local government is the result of lively and varied growth over a long period. It has, in the British way, always cared more for vitality than for mechanical regularity, and it is best considered, not merely as a piece of machinery, but as part of a living organism. Its function has been to give the citizen a chance of self-government at his own level, and at each stage of its history it has represented an intermediate stage of government between the central executive and himself' (*Post-War Britain 1946*, p. 9).

By 1971, the emphasis was less on organic growth and more on how the system was comprehensive and statute-based. The current view also reflected Redcliffe-Maud and other proposals for change:

'Government on a local basis has been part of the administrative system of the United Kingdom for many centuries. In its present shape much of it dates back to the late nineteenth century, when the conception of a comprehensive system of locally elected councils to manage various services provided for the benefit of the community was first incorporated in statute law. Since that time there has been a large increase in the population, and a massive transformation in the range, complexity and scale of local authority functions. Because of this, local government in Greater London was reorganised in the 1960s and radical changes in the structure in England and Scotland have been proposed' (*Britain 1971*, p. 67).

Debating local government in the House of Commons in 1995, one minister emphasised the financial importance of local government and the need for efficiency:

'One-fifth of all Government expenditure is spent by local authorities. Central Government support through the revenue support grant is roughly equivalent to 10p on the standard rate of income tax. It is vital, therefore, that we should concentrate on local government. It is not often that we concentrate on 20 per cent of government expenditure in one debate. The proper conduct of local authorities means that resources should be well used. It means also that priorities should be set according to genuine need. It means further that waste and bureaucracy should be cut' (*Hansard*, Volume 262, Number 129, col 1151).

List of Abbreviations

CCT	compulsory competitive tendering
CEMR	Council of European Municipalities and Regions
DLO	direct labour organisation
DSO	direct service organisation
EU	European Union
GLC	Greater London Council (dissolved 1986)
HRA	housing revenue account
IULA	International Union of Local Authorities
LCC	London County Council (dissolved 1965)
LGIB	Local Government International Bureau
NNDR	national non-domestic rate
SCA	supplementary credit approval
SSA	standard spending assessment

Addresses

Department of the Environment, 2 Marsham Street, London SW1P 3EB.

Northern Ireland Office, Parliament Buildings, Stormont Castle, Belfast BT4 3ST.

The Scottish Office, New St Andrew's House, Edinburgh EH1 3TG.

Welsh Office, Cathays Park, Cardiff CF1 3NQ.

Department for Education and Employment, Sanctuary Buildings, Great Smith Street, London SW1P 3BT.

Department of Health, Richmond House, 79 Whitehall, London SW1A 2NS.

Department of Transport, 2 Marsham Street, London SW1P 3EB.

Home Office, 50 Queen Anne's Gate, London SW1H 9AT.

Association of County Councils, 66a Eaton Square, London SW1W 9BH.

Association of District Councils, Chapter House, 26 Chapter Street, London SW1P 4NP.

Association of Local Authorities of Northern Ireland, 123 York Street, Belfast BT15 1AB.

Association of London Government, 36 Old Queen Street, London SW1H 9HP.

Association of Metropolitan Authorities, 34 Great Smith Street, London SW1P 3BJ.

Audit Commission, 1 Vincent Square, London SW1P 2PN.

Commission for Local Administration in England:

General enquiries plus London, Kent, East Sussex and West Sussex:
21 Queen Anne's Gate, London SW1H 9BU.

East Anglia, the South West, the west, the south and most of central England:
The Oaks, Westwood Way, Westwood Business Park, Coventry CV4 8JB.

The East Midlands and the north of England:
Beverley House, 17 Shipton Road, York YO3 6FZ.

Commission for Local Authority Accounts, 18 George Street, Edinburgh EH2 2QU.

Convention of Scottish Local Authorities, Roseberry House, 9 Haymarket Terrace, Edinburgh EH12 5XZ.

Local Government Commission for England, Dolphyn Court, 10–11 Great Turnstile, Lincoln's Inn Fields, London WC1V 7JU.

Local Government International Bureau, 35 Great Smith Street, London SW1P 3BJ.

National Association of Local Councils, 109 Great Russell Street, London WC1B 3LD.

Further Reading

The Citizen's Charter: Raising the Standard. Cm 1599. ISBN 0 10 115992 7.	HMSO	1991	£8.50
The Conduct of Local Authority Business: the Government Response to the Report of the Widdicombe Committee of Inquiry. Cm 433. ISBN 0 10 1043225.	HMSO	1988	£5.90
Local Government Financial Statistics England No 4 1990/91–1993/94. ISBN 0 11 752900 1.	HMSO	1993	£11.50
Local Government Ground Rules R. J. B. Morris. ISBN 0 582 07151 8.	Longman	1990	£22.00
Local Government in Britain Tony Byrne. Sixth edition. ISBN 0 14 017663 2.	Penguin Books	1994	£10.00
The Local Government System Peter G. Richards. ISBN 0 04 352105 3.	George Allen and Unwin	1983	
Local Government Today A. Chandler. ISBN 0 7190 3296 2.	Manchester University Press	1991	£9.90

Municipal Yearbook.
Annual report   Municipal Journal Ltd

Parish and Town Councils in England:
a Survey, by Sheila Ellwood,
Sandra Nutley, Mike Tricker and
Piers Waterson.
ISBN 0 11 752592 8.   HMSO   1992   £9.00

Report of the Committee of Inquiry
into the Conduct of Local Authority
Business. Chairman:
Mr David Widdicombe QC.
Cmnd 9797. ISBN 0 10 197970 3.   HMSO   1993   £12.50

Index

Printed in the UK for HMSO.
Dd.302169, 4/96, C30, 566734, 5673, 345774.